Love Hieroglyphics

Iris Yanette Seda

Copyright © 2016 Iris Yanette Seda
All rights reserved.
ISBN-13:
978-1537589312

ISBN-10:
1537589318

Dedication

I dedicate this book to my father Antonio Seda for believing and always encouraging me to follow my dreams, accomplish my goals and live to the fullest of my potential. I also want to dedicate this accomplishment to my mother: Francisca Rodriguez and my kids: Angela Emerson, Abraham Sepulveda, Amanda Sepulveda, Anna Sepulveda and Dalia Cortes and daughter in law Taiesha Edwards; as I want them to learn that age is irrelevant to goals and dreams. Life is far more enjoyable and challenging when fighting to make our dreams factual manifestations of our desires, despite of time and age. We live only once, let's cramp all the possible living in between intervals of combat and make our dreams come true. Dreams are stars that can be reached and touched. I want to thank you, dad and thank you, kids for all your support and encouragement throughout every single one of my life's endeavors. It has really touched my heart and blessed me dearly.

ACKNOWLEDGMENTS

I want to thank my father Antonio Seda for always believing in me and teaching me to believe in myself. I want to thank my kids for encouraging me to fulfill my dreams. I also want to thank my closest friends for believing in me, encouraging me and supporting my dreams, goals and aspirations. I am truly and humbly thankful for you, all.

Sonia Richards (RIP) and Jennifer Lacina (RIP)

Gloria Bell, Aynesia Bell, Nic Harris, Maxine Hines,

Elia Rosado, Irma Rosado, Robin Gilchrist, Rafael Torres and Rafael Febus y su Francisca

CONTENTS

Acknowledgments		V
1	Praises to the Almighty	1
2	As Love Inspires	6
3	Self-Love, Womanly	15
4	Once Upon a Poet Lover	26
5	Lust in Love	39
6	Losing Love's Melancholies	54
7	In Love with Nature	71
8	Because Love is Raising Awareness	88

1 PRAISES TO THE ALMIGHTY

Liquid Blessings

I stand in the bridge of the waterfall
and by its crystal glare, as it seems to call.

Margined by obedience, I hold the hand
that takes me to the throne of the Lamb.

Responding to him, I walk by the river trail
towards the steamy voice that at me wails.

I feel God's misty spirit and begin to cry;
I sense His presence from beneath the sky.

Given the symbolic gift of His resurrection,
I submerge in waters to declare my salvation.

Humbly meek, an obedient step is expressed.
for His love for humanity He has professed.

By His cleansing blood our sins are undone,
for He so loved us, that He gave us His son.

For his baptismal river, I give Him the praise
for His pure love and for the gift of His grace.

God in a Song

When caught in the middle of the storm
Where nothing seems to make sense
When life seems dark, almost deformed
And this pain is too dense
To be reminded that in you I can be strong

When I'm brought to my knees by life's lessons
When I lose the purpose of these internal abrasions
When I'm at wits ends unable to survive
And I'm way too tired to fight and strive

When fears come to tear myself apart
Even though I know you hold my heart

Ever so kindly you show your face
And through lyrics I find your grace

I find your healing in the words of a song
And I find myself whispering them along
I have to sing and cry for restoration
With surrendering determination
So you can heal these inflictions and abrasions

Every note and every beat
Carries me away from this defeat
Turning all my bitterness manna sweet
And I see your face of love and mercy
Rebuking away, all of these disturbing frenzies

God it is you I hear, so loud and clear
God You are so real that I can feel you near

When all seems to fall apart
With a song you heal my heart
I hear your voice in the myths of wailing winds
I feel and see you, as impossible as it seems

Every note and every beat
Carries me away from this defeat
Turning all my bitterness manna sweet
And I see your face of love and mercy
Smiling away, all of these disturbing frenzies

God, it is you I hear, so loud and clear
God, You are so real that I can feel you near

When caught in the middle of the storm
Where nothing seems to make sense
When life seems dark, almost deformed
And this pain is too dense
I can always find you in a song

God in Bloom

Sometimes, I walk the bridge and stand there,
simply going into an introspective spindrift.
I am carried away by the symphonic crashing of waves
and the blowing and bellowing winds.
Lost in a meditative stance of this passionate pilgrimage,
I breathe in the sultry memories of moments like these.
Passed the din of drivers and passers-by
in sight, I reach the distant boundless mountains
of the early blooming horizon.
I stand in its summit yearning to gaze upon God's home,
through this heaven's veil blue curtain.
And I do!
There at the very top of the bridge I've walked so many
times before.
I can always find the marvelous rich nourishments of
mother natures as a love gift from God Himself.

Commanding Mountains to Move

Upon pacing the parquet flooring of my cold room,
my discalced intuition absorbs the bone penetrating chills
that hint the autumn of my life.

A stampede of stagnation rhythmically gallops through
the russet fields of my mind, where the mountains are crimson
and scarlet.

Where is peace? Where is love? Where is my life?

Unreachable perhaps,
At the burgundy cellophane summit and under the canvass of
Gray sky.
 Unmoved
By the halted voice of absently serene primroses and fresh love
orchids.

And time…

Time waves ocher tones and yellow undertones to sight
Of transformation's needs, as I levitate from my body.
I travel in spirit toward the shallow water of semantics
Screaming shattered the halted silence with a loud command:

Move mountains, move!

My soul screams from the superficial currents of my faith.
And there, at that instant, from within the shaded semblance
Of those large mountains, the sun begins to rise
And the mountains to move.

And all I had to do was command them to, in Jesus name.

The Word Beyond Rationalization

Through an unknown preacher, the spirit quotes me,
leaving me in reflection of his earnest words.
Beyond my very own understanding, You emancipate
a response to my rebelliousness, through the vessel of
a sermon.
Ever so gently, you rebuke the obstinacies I spoke,
minutes ago. A preacher's word became prime evidence
of your gifts of spiritual anointments and a proven experience
of your transcending power. No, it is not coincidental!
-It is faith, beyond rationalizations.-It is belief beyond conception.
-It is proof beyond hesitation.
Despite others' perceptive myths of His lack of existence,
I am summoned to believe.

God's Winged Petals

Fairytale cocoons are the sanctuary lodges of heaven's maidens.
Miraculously transformed into Cinderellas of the sky.
They live to fly like petals in the wind, even in just briefly.
Majestic, their sight us a fragmented momentum of enchanted
Godly loving graces, as they hover over grassy fields and
Flowered meadows.
Coquettes of colorful array and peaceful glide,
Butterflies are but the nectar truth of God's existence.

There is God!

He is in the dear sight of a new born child
and in the marigold that are growing wild.

He is rooted in the love of our mothers
and in the words of a caring brothers.

He is in the notes and voice of a gospel song
and in the chirping of birds singing along.

He is in the comforting words of a friend
and in the words of one making amends.

He is in the skillful doctor's healing hands
and within the faith that a placebo demands.

He is the convicting sermon of a preacher
and within the loving kindness of a teacher.

He is in the oxygen that feeds our lives
and in the strength that feeds our strives.

He is the emerald colors of our fruitful lands
and in the plunging waves that wash the sand.

He is in the sweat-full harvest of falls crops
and in the scented moisture of spring dew drops.

He is in summer's playfully natured heat
and in cold winter's white covered streets.

He is in the wisdom of time making us gray
and the mighty power that washes sins away.

He is the son of God dying for our salvation
and in the blood that makes us a new creation.

He is in the rhyme of this poetical profession
and in the answers to all of our questions.

2 AS LOVE INSPIRE

Elysium Pebbled Pathway

I will pebble the pathway
to the prophesy of our love;
just follow the trail
of wild florets
and the crimson dawn.

There
under the red sky
and among the forest passion
of my flesh is paradise.

I am not a fairytale,
nor am I a legend,

just a mere woman calling you
into a dream drift
with my siren's song.

Let my voice draw you
to the Elysium
where the honeysuckles mist
of my passion is
your only sustenance.

Love me
from the brick red tones above
until
the evanescent sapphire veils
the whole sky.

Become touch,
caress
and the voice of earth
whispering in my ear,
while I voicelessly indulge
in the music box rhythm
of your body dancing on mine.

Permanently engrave your being
to mine,
sketch your passions on me
and carve your name on my flesh.

Love me
from the birth of our first primavera
to the dusk of many winters to come.
For I am simply yours!

Another Gypsy Legend

Side walking the lush woodlands
and the meadowy lagoon
they've crossed path again and again.
Undeniably their crossed gaze
spoke of a forbidden love
of fruitless endeavor.

Nomadic the wanderer struggled
to remain kindred to her people
yet untrue to her heart.

Under a moment of weakness
and intense seduction
he took what was rightfully his.
-Her heart.

They gave into the carnal concession
that consumed and bent their will.
Tranced by her bronzed skin
and the seductive aroma
of her curled onyx hair
he undressed her scarlet robes
and fed from her virginal mystique.

Lavished by his manliness she was weakened
by the canvassed mischief of his touch.
For a moment forbearance was tossed aside
and replaced by a susceptive provocation
of a lustrous moment.

Drunken and intoxicated
by her spell casting beauty, he went home.

Her taunted by the impossibility of their feelings
casted herself into the lagoon's depth
and was unheard from ever again.

Broken and bewilder by the news
he went after her and did the same.

Today, it is said that under the full moon
you can see them dancing
upon the glistening sight of the lagoon
and if you're very still
you may hear in the waving water
the mysterious sound of her voice.

<u>Reassuring The Apprehension</u>

Apprehensive yet observant
you lurk like a spy on my intentions.
Defensive with a coping mechanism
you fear building sand castles;
as do I.

Life is an unwarranted dream catcher.
It is not up to me,
nor up to you.
Cast away your fear and toss mine along.

I offer you not pain,
nor deceit, but true love.
Quiet your doubts.
They are but suspicious qualms
confusing your mind.

Let your apprehensive eyes open
to see what my heart holds for you.
Let your hands harvest
the fruit of my love vow.

Let your heart love again.
Let your being be loved.

But above all,
let God show you His will for us.

Apprehension is but a game
of the enemy.
Can't you see?

I hand you the serene reassurance
of a promise built
on the foundation of God's will.

Unequivocally, lets build our castle
on Him and not on our desires.

I'll submissively beckon after you
as I am called to do.
Will you?

Hesitance Kiss

Your lips are a mystery I yearn to decipher,
a most desired clandestine secret
I long to discover.
Expectation abound,
I swim the sea of the indecisiveness
that prevents me from savoring them.
Upon the shore of their dulcet taste,
their sugar still a secrecy
belonging to no one but you.

Undress your selfish withdrawal
and share their lotus
for this feverish desideratum is my death.
Let me kiss the seal of my love promise
upon their voluptuous
yet delicately aligned apprehension.
For just one kiss, will make you forever mine.

Spartan Love in Prose

He had no weakness but the gleaming brown
of her eyes and the softness of her amber hair.
Enchanted by the regal presence of her warrior,
she felt the same. They were a perfect consummation
of a veiled love.

With her soft kiss, she tamed his furies and with
her love making, she blazed his outmost lustful
burning rages. She was the calmed fury that kept
him clear headed at combat.

Death was never an option. Honor was to return
victorious to toast to the intoxicating drink of her
sweat. Strong yet reverent to the woman that held
his heart, words were never necessary, nor permissible.
There was no room for weaknesses.

In the loud silent embrace his greatest conquest was
their love. -And they both new it.

On Visual Dialogues

He looked at me with unrecognizable eyes.
-Eyes which swelled me up
and flickered something within that slept
peaceful, yet in hibernating wait.

Then, he spoke his first words to me
totally captivating me at first sight.
Though it hasn't been long since we first met,
we feel right to one another;
we fit together like a perfect jigsaw puzzle.

Every day is a new adventure,
-the beginning of a voyage I am yielding to
sail heart at hand.
A heart he already calls his own.

He looked at me with those unrecognizable eyes,

Now, I can proficiently read.
And I, I just love what they say to me.

Poetic Exchange

Though poetry is a language we both speak
 and we could be the perfect soul lovers;
 sometimes love is just meant to be felt,
 it is just meant to be a muse...

Jasper Fantasy

Among the myths of fadeless fantasies,
my maiden fairy ardently dances
to the lavender gleam of rippled currents.

She tenderly dashes Purple topaz,
jasper and tanzanite gems among the
undulating crystallized liquid lilac,

where she waltzes upon
conjuring my spirit on a journey,
aloofly, where she haphazardly for me waits.

There, where the incantation of her magic
looms and the moon covetously watches her
dance is where I belong.

She brings me home to her in chimera chariots
of thistle fairy dust while I dream myself
undoing her silk gown and running my finger
through her velvet soft hair.

-Losing my lips upon the arched jugular
softness that has always allured me
insane.

Dance, my fairy maiden dance,
I'll soon be there.

Sometimes Love

Sometimes destiny makes the choice for us.
Still I think you are meant to be.
Still I think we are **meant** to be.

Sometimes surrendering onto love's beaconing
 is where we find what we did not see come.
 -True Love

Chimerically Found

Follow its rhythms
Every beat will guide you to me
-A chimera of sprouting feelings
Wanting to become devotions
Hear me, I am found

The Lips of My Rose

Her lips were sweet.
They were even sweeter
When they spoke my name
Or sought mine with such wants
That made avoidance of these feelings
Futile.

I became adept at reading them,
I read even the silent words
hidden behind the spoken ones.

And there was something about
The way her top lip curved when upset
That impassioned me with lust melting disputes
Into the dew of reconciliation.

Her smile was enough to bring me a peace
I longed for and became my placebo and bloom.

Her lips today are the memories

Of a tender winter where roses
Bloomed at whims and threaded
The velvet of sweet love making.

Bridal Slumber

At the sublime edge
of excelsis benediction
we are now one in name.
You are mine and I am yours.

A chambered ballad
is the ambiance
your gown dances to
as you walk.

Wanting to preserve
the purity of my Madonna
I withhold my wanton
desires
while enjoying
the delicate joy of true love.

Silently imploding
I breathe the fragrance
of the skin I softly caress,
mutely surveying the curves
that have brought me
to paradise.

We glide into matters of
the heart becoming
physically one,
/now/
threading our bodies into
the soul bond fabric
of love making.

At the cusp of purity
I claim her woman first.

Once webbed on white silk

surrender exhaustion comes
upon her, while I watch
my bride slumber.
Sleep my love,
sleep.

I am watching over you.

Refugee of His Embrace

after a maniacal chastised
lust slumber
I fall into the serenity
of a casting care embrace

his

where buoyantly my pneuma
only finds rest
and my flesh is tamed
with silent somnolent kisses

by a melodious warm snooze
of palpitations
I am a refugee

between the arms
of him
who holds me until
the dawning raven's song

3 SELF-LOVE, WOMANLY

True Currency

woman don't forget your worth
discounts of self are but future grievances
future disappointing tears

don't allow the loneliness to make you forget
that you are someone's answer to a prayer

a priceless prize
not to be bought with lies and empty promises
but with action that speak otherwise

actions that speak of want, care and commitment
anything less is an unaffordable expense of self

woman don't forget your worth
flaunt it
and scream it for even the selectively deafened
to hear that
love is the only true currency for you

A Real Woman

A real woman
does not look to make profit of a man,
but hustles for her own
and know the importance of merging
growth efforts with her companion.

A real woman
does not seek validation in a man;
she already knows her worth
and lives a virtuously
and self-respecting life.

A real woman does not measure
herself against the next,
instead she encourages another
woman to become her best.

A real woman
does not engage in childish games,
for she is able to lovingly convey
her wants and needs.

A real woman
is never unfaithful;
she values her companion
and does onto him as
she wishes done onto herself.

A real woman
is not lazy; nor does she makes
excuses for her short comings.
She rather wakes with dawn, seeds
and harvests the sweat of her brow.

A real woman
is not selfish
she shows her love in her giving
in sharing her provisions without
expectations.

A real woman
is never directionless;
for she brings all to the altar
in praise and thanksgiving
and follows the light shone
to her feet.

A real woman
is not dull;
the beauty of her soul
speaks and glistens like stars
of truth through her eyes.

A real woman
is simply the art and the action

of being who she truly is
in self-love.

I'm a Voice in Prose

the soft call of the wind,
a sensual summon,
an angered statement,
a boiling revolution, a grief,
a lost, a love, a passion,
a woman

I am a voice in prose

controversial, real, impacting,
evocative of anger,
other times sweet, gentle
and even enthralling
but always
the woman I am

I am a voice in prose

at the rhythms of experiences
and life's lessons,
the free verse of desires,
wants and yearnings
the metaphoric sounds
of pain,
lack and the paralyzing
strength of my
womanly fears

I am a voice in prose

hear it and see me through it
understand it and learn me
from it
embrace it and you will
experience the love
respect it and I will
reciprocate

hate it and you will see
this woman
not give a damn

I am a voice in prose

the innermost reverse
the aura of my canvas
inside out
mental synopsis of an opened book
outlines of a life
all that I am
the woman I've become

I am a voice in prose

sometimes a bit of a cliché
but never a carbon copy
other time mediocre
as I am still under construction
learning each and every day
at its best tugging hearts,
and evoking emotions
but always me

the voice a woman in prose

Erected Silhouette

Tender bloom, I walk my fingers to tease the springs blossomed into the erected crest, where the lips of tenderness latch and feed from.

They are sustenance!

Voluptuous and fertile are the mountains of femininity and soft is the feathered caress of their nurturing power.

They are liquid verve!

Delicious are the pearled springs of life erupting from within their volcanic nipplets.

They are nourishment!

They are simply the blissful silhouette of life, engorged and perfectly incarnated by creation.

They are life!

Womanly Alliteration

Woman, you're all too familiar with new beginnings.
Why do you fear?

Woman, you know all too well the pain of lost, you've survive it!

Woman, you have strived and have conquered.
Be encouraged, you could do this!

Woman, you have loved with all your might.
Love yourself!

Woman, you have created and brought forth life.
You're the vessel of existence.

Woman, you have raised and guided our future.
Walk the walk…

Woman, you're mother earth's sister.
Love your family.

Woman, you've fought and won many battles.
Keep jabbing!

Woman, you're strength is an example to many.
Strive and climb mightily.

Woman, your Father, God is a king.
Claim your royalty.

Woman, a man's rib was needed to create you.
Love and teach our sons to do the same.

Woman, you're a most beautiful being,
just believe what you see within and without.
Believe in yourself!

C'mon Woman

C'mon woman love yourself a little!

Look within and see the fruitful
promise that you are. Allow
that found assurance to rebuke
the lack of self-esteem that
obfuscate your true self.

C'mon woman love yourself a little!

Look upon the constellation and
find awe in the creation that you are;
not to be used, abused or taken for
granted but to be loved, cared for
and respected.

C'mon woman love yourself a little!

Look at your attractive prominence
and find the internal beauty that
makes you a unique being and set aside
all erroneous outer-validation ideas.

C'mon woman love yourself a little!

Look at your worth and do not settle
for being second best in love affairs
but hold your standards high as
you are great uxorial material.

C'mon woman love yourself a little!

Look upon society and be that
productive member full of affable
fertile plans of growth, craft a better
world for yours by being
professionally proactive.

C'mon woman love yourself a little!

Look upon your goals and do not fear
the climb to the summit, for your God
has given you a bravado spirit of
strength as tool for success.

C'mon woman love yourself a little!

Look upon the meaning of these words
of encouragement and strive with
all your might to be the woman,
you are meant to be.

C'mon woman love yourself a little!

Look at the mirroring reflection
of this parable and see yourself
smiling back!

Morphed Womanhood

Sappily, once am month I lose myself.
The joys of womanhood make me feel vulnerable
And sentimental, those days.

Bloated with emotions, sadness and annoyance
My soul is heavier to me.
My pants can't fit the refluxed annoyance
Of everyday stimuli.
-noises,
Stupid questions,
The damn dishes
And everything these days bring.

Unsatisfied,

Carbs and chocolate comforts me not.
Nothing seem to, anyhow...
Emotional...
Today,
I am just PMSing monster.

Exuding Femininity

Conceived
and vessel of conception
she is far more than the sustenance of survival.
Time and time again rebirthing herself,
she has surpassed a sense of utterance complacence.
She has evolved beyond the Neanderthal behaviors
that still linger in modern society.
Despite shackled taboos
and restrictions she still wears the soft silk gowns
of pulchritude, self-respect and decorum.
She manages to be a professional diplomat
of euphemism
and still make her point across.
Though perception may nominate her
a bitch,
her strength is in her beliefs and accomplishments.
-But also in her beauty and docile feminine refinement.
Never a weaker vessel,
she is also the embodiment of love and a lover.
In that sentiment, she is instinctively protective
yet pleasantly possessive.
She is a burning bush of sensuality amidst.
She is beauty.
She is intelligence.
She is a conqueror.
She is simply a woman.

Mujer

Mujer,
 Look at yourself with gentle eyes
 In the objective mirror of self-validation
 Because accepting who you really are

Is worth the aches of self-exploration

Mujer,
Do not let the social strata conjugate your
Real beauty with marketing manipulations
For such search for the perfect physical
Image is a lamentable dehumanization

Mujer,
Your fragility's scars speak of strength
Yet all you see is self-esteem bruises
But, unfortunately, those that don't
Understand, only see reasons as excuses

Mujer,
Once again, I urge you to ignore the
Slandering critics' lack of acceptance
For the only unpleasant ugliness is their
Perceptively unrealistic extravagance

Mujer,
Rise above all and become the vessel
Of life, you are meant to be to the world
You're meant to shine from within your
Inner beauty, not to be a mockingbird

Little Girl at Heart

Watching Sponge Bob
On a cold Sunday morning
Under my wool bed covers
The child in me warming.
I am a big kid at heart
There is no other way to live
For life alone can be harsh
Enough to our joy thieve

Jacquanna

Her onyx eyes are two magnetic pendulums
that physically draw you into her sadden void
and though her red lips exaltingly distract

her clear melancholy a seer cannot avoid

Red Lips Concealments

Hidden vulnerabilities wear a red smile
In delicate high heels walking for miles
Tired sometimes bruised she still blooms
Despite all the aches that at her loom
She will continue to walk and to fight
Against her woes with all of her might
Just because giving up isn't an option
She continues to live heeding caution
Smiling crimson what it's concealed
-A melancholy that cannot be revealed

Discalced Becoming

Calloused feet have walked discalced
Both the good and the bad of her choices
And she has verbalized many experiences
Through her poetical muses and voices

Wisdom has painted her gray like
The colored path she chose to walk on
But the options to choose from, were bruised
Black, blues and not white like cotton

But she has lived, endured and rebirthed
To the being she is because of it all
She has few regrets but has survived
All of the hell that her life recalled

Though her life never smelled like roses
She has no expectation for empathy
For experiences have taught her
To accepts no allowances of sympathy

Calloused feet have walked discalced
And have learned from her choices
Thus she celebrates the woman she's
Become though these muses and voices

Resilience Becomes Her

She discovered a resilience within
Never known to her before
A strength that me her feel excised
And rebirthed from her very core
The legend of the Phoenix fell short
Of the glory of her reconciliation
For the peace and tranquility, she
Learned was her reincarnation

On Womanly Morals

Self-respect and prudence are
never outdated or out of style.
I am just stating my opinion,
I am not meaning to profile.

4 ONCE UPON A POET LOVER

Spellbound

witchery is falling in love, so forget
all you thought you knew about gravity
is to yield oneself into the dulcet lotus
of loving and all of its unconventionality

a bitter sweet brewery of a shaman aloof
whom mantras are rock and roll
rhythmically rhyming a spell by
pricking verbal needles into my soul

True Profession

True, you cannot see the substance
of these feeling to you I profess.
Seeing your doubts makes me
apprehensive, thus make me recess.

But I'll try to understand that is normal
to feel apprehension sometimes
and not interpret them as red flags
or no type of warning sign.

Instead, I will still love you through
these emotional hurtles and doubts
and prove to you with actions
the substance of what you arouse.

So, don't let these feelings make
you retreat from what I want to give
open your mind and your heart
and be willing to be loved and live.

Take a chance on me I promise
not to ever let you down.
The ball is in your court
you can either love or shutdown.

But be assured that this love
I speak of is really real
but I won't force my love on you
shame how doubt good loving steals

Your Zen

Sometimes recovery comes with
red lipstick and a whip for a pen,
promising to help heal a battered spirit
with her body as placebo and Zen.

Wearily, you question the future,
well baby, it can only be made.
When you're weak, I'll be strong.
When I'm weak, you'll do the trade.

So please let me love you,
if that is all, I can physically do
and with lovingly kind actions
your faith in the future renew.

Writing Our Love

Love and time are allies of the laureate
writing the chapters of our lives.
So, I will turn poems into petals
and let these muses be my drive.

For I am the calligraphist of my own
emotions, desires and choices.
Thus, I aim to poetically translate,
love and time into rhyming voices.

They echo like aloof drums in mantras
distinctively calling our names,
rhythmically dancing and singing,
as I poetically translate their claims.

Open Invitation

Want to be the answer to my poetical pleas
and cross through our destiny's door?.
Surf the waves of time to me and come to
where the sun dawns, upon a beach shore.

Good Morning Love

Seductions awaken by the first sun ray's kiss
thus the world's lovers are baptized by dawn's bliss

It Will Be What Is Meant to Be!

Will it be winter? Will it be spring?
Will it be a season that my lover brings?
Will it be night time or will it be morning?
Will it be under the sun of midmorning?
Will it be sunny or will it be raining?
Will it be evanescent or will it be sustaining?
Will it be sweet or intimidating?
Will it be tenderly soft or fiery and intoxicating?
Will it be a romance of tequila sunshines?
Will it be quality proof of its universal design?

Ponderings

pendulous drums play a mantra aloof
his words echoing through poetry alludes
between a concealed language of bodies
never concealing the enrapture to nobody
coyly teasing with such a captivating yen
but only the sun really knows when
all these metaphors will become actions
and we can give into such mutual attractions
Yes, I guess the sun and time will tell
when we as one are to dwell

Love Like His

He loves me ever so sweetly and tender,
 beaconing me to him totally rendered.
 Oh, but his love is so passionate, I don't mind.
 -Never knew love of such kind.

Mused

he is good for my muse
by his words I am infused
by these desires to communicate
and imagery conjugate
how I yearn having him near
instead messages to him I smear
little love notes and clues
to tell him, he is good for my muse

Chariot of Time

beaconed and yielded, I walk to you with
spilling fears overflowing from my hands
like levitating through some magnetic field
pulled by a force I can't begin to understand

as something so beautiful is birthing and
blooming to roses despite winter weather
despite the measure of distance, a time's
chariot promises to bring us together

Proverbial Travel

Travel through my dreams and meet me
where we can love one another.
So we can satiate all the yen far beyond
poetry and proverbs.

Quarreling In Rhyme

Evocative power is capable of conveying the
 most powerful of points with the silk of imagery;
even quarreling in the myths of rhyme are for the
 eyes of whom can infer and extrapolate, literally.

Spun In Love

I am caught in your centrifuge spin
where my atoms are separating
where I'm tossed into a whirlpool and
my spirit from my body is oscillating

Rolling Dices on Us

No longer do I need to crave the aches of loss,
no more additions of weight onto my cross.
Instead, I claim a promise of future kisses,
of abundant growth and harvesting blisses.
For once, I'm strong enough to choose love instead
and to no longer live life holding by a thread.
-But taking a chance and a leap onto destiny
 Because I know this could work, I feel the chemistry.
 So I give myself permission to love again
  some' tells me: "Take the chance, It won't be in vain"

Roses and Wine

Roses bloom at the brink of a fantasy.
Wine and cheers to such rhapsody!

This Is Real

When the nightly slumber merges
with these unsought feelings,
even they feel like lies.
Loneliness disguises as lies

like helium balloons just floating
on the empty nocturnal air.
But when the morning sun
rises and kisses my cheek with
the first thought of you
I know this is real.

The Power of His Voice

a cymbal echoing in her mind
was the tone of his voice
it had power to penetrate her whole
leaving her vulnerable
to a lustful enthrallment
a chosen state of confinement
his voice commanded
her ghouls and skeletons
rebuked and exiled
and he became a resident there
his voice was that compelling
that hypnotically persuasive
that she levitated in a yielded
will, right into his arms

Found

Feeling found
intrinsically you're inexplicably
in me, at a cellular level.
We are one, quantumly.

Benedictine Placebo

I can conjugate him as the recovery
Of my deepest afflictions,
And the words of his poems a
As placebo and healing benediction.

Loving My Troubadour

My troubadour of verbal caresses
To whom my devotions professes

Give your nomadic love yens to me
So a nebbish love story we can conceive

Yielding to this intoxicating pheremonal call
To the primal refluxes we're both enthralled

Make love to me through your muse's persuasion
Start fore-playing with your verbal transmutations

My troubadour, sing me, your poems conspicuously
So I can follow your lyrics yielded and capriciously

Into the forever type of love affair, you offer
And into the love that to one another, we proffer

Rest In Our Love

Rest on my chest your lonesome slumber
And in my bosom satisfy the hunger
That you have felt to be loved and wanted
And not to ever be taken you for grated
I felt the same, and our wait is over
And to make this love we have the power
Come to me, my love, sleep upon my chest
And put these lonely feelings of ours to rest

How Can You?

How can you say I care not for your poetry
when I can see is the door to your spirit?
When your words are the threshold
I cross to your love in every lyric?

How can you say I care not for your poetry
when that is how I come to know of you?

When they entrance me to beacon after
You in such wooing pursues?

How can you say I care not for your poetry,
When I am in love with the poet you are?
When they are the very lyrics you've
Written to play on your guitar?

How can you say I care not for your poetry?
When I learn you through your poetry pieces?
Wow! I must admit that you thinking I care not
has rendered me speechless.

The Way I Feel

You are in a place in my heart in which,
If I was to lose you, I would surely lose myself.
Those are my true feelings in rhyme the way
You like, not just a vase to place on a shelf.

I will say this again; I only want you.
And please don't take my words lightly.
I am a darn good woman, never a whore
And I cannot say this much more politely.

Yet on that very same breath of muse
I say that I have much to learn.
I mean not to disrespect you
I hope that, you can discern.

Poetical Caresses

I want to kiss you with the poetic lips
Of this love's affirmations
And reach you so profoundly that
We become a touchless consummation

All I can do in hope of reaching you
Through imageries and scribes
But this feeling is committedly stronger
That any words can describe

Rendered impotently speechless
I can only attempt to tell you in rhymes
That I would have never met someone
Like you in a million life times

And now that your so close
Even despite of the distance
I become fearful when sensing
Your passive resistance

And I fear you leaving me
Though I am not a location or place
Because something things and people
Are also left and displaced.

If we could only make love
To these mutual apprehensions
But we're simply tied up to
Place and time dimensions

Allow yourself to be caressed
By the touchless hands of my muse
Until the very time of our union when
With this love we can be literally infused

Our Love

There is a love breathing in existence
Despite its lover's physical distance
There is a love aloofly singing songs
About a place afar where it belongs
There is a love oozing desires in prose
And rhyme for its lovers to compose
There is a love in verb being portrayed
In subtle parabolas waiting to be made

Whimsical Connotations

Immersive parabolas beacon me into
An illustrious magnetic pull,

As his words are hypnotic forces of
An exponential poetic whirlpool

These whimsy manifestations are
Simple muses that can't be compared
Spoken revelations which are
The equivalence of our love affair

They paint and color a love
That may cause other's consternation
Of unexplainable dreams come true
Written in muses of a connotation

So let us write our whimsical
Intricacies in emboldened letters
So they can portrait impassionedly
Our reciprocate romantic endeavors

Waxing Moon and Womanly Awakened

No longer emotionally hibernating
I am a waxing moon
Intuitively coloring silver, the sky
With my heart finally attuned

Solemnly allowing myself
To feel this conquered adoration
Profoundly receiving and
Reciprocating these admirations

No longer emotionally hibernating
I am a tequila sunrise in bloom
Doing away with doubt's fears corpses
Leaving them unburied and exhumed

Thus, I love him wholly, immune
to the poisons of apprehensions
awaken to these womanly feelings
I am no longer in hibernation

Mercurial Taunting

Mercurial energies like lava's rise
Erupting in pleasure of a carnal nature
Of a desire and yen my spirit, soul
And woman within so need to nurture.

Monopolizing longings crotchet me his;
Interconnecting us into a most perfect want
Of irresistibly mutual fostered urges
Into an enchantment that tenderly taunts

Sardonically Proverbial

His sardonic fire is a verbal reverie
Of contemptuous satire spoken so cleverly.

His poems can sometimes be rapaciously idealistic
As his voice is indigenously and consciously ritualistic.

The voice of ancestry through him speaks a tongue
Of proverbial grievances which have echoed and rung.

Endurance Summon

Time and distance to lovers
are but endurance's tests.
The ups and downs that when
we love, we welcome abreast.

Billowed into the nontraditional
They still pursue the feeling in common.
They surrender to the ambuscade of a
Love, by which they have been summoned.

Serenity

His verbal acumen pacifies me tenderly,
entrances me and composes me serene.

Reconciling my pneuma to harmony from
the mindless madness of the everyday routine.

He, Oxymoron

If I was to try to explain the way
her affects me, I would be speechless.
because he is all, my muses, my silences
my strength and my weakness.

Touchless Impressions

He unknowingly bends my soul
Bent like weeping willows
And I feel his summoned butterflies
Hovering over floral meadows

His mantras cast my cleavage
Into a dancing palpitation
Becoming the pure oxygen to
To infuse my fleshed respiration

Oh yeah, he does me touchless
Without a hint of suspicion
Of how his manly claims in me
Are making an impression

Rhyming Dialogues

I rhyme the humility of his affections
Because, they are a metaphorical infusion.

Esoterically, he muses so exclusive
Emotions felt ever so obtrusive.

He speaks our love in riddles so tenderly.
Truthfully, we can both rhyme it, endlessly.

But when he speaks, he melts me puddle,
With words that to others may muddle.

We quote in rhymes random conversations
Hard sometimes to outer interpretation.

Our poetical muses are attracting magnets
Able to rhyme and precipitate the most stagnate.

Imprudently Primal

Satiate the imprudent summon of
This uncultured lust spoken in a thresh
For me, there is no diplomacy when
The primal speaks acclaimed the flesh

Satiate the imprudent summon of
This uncultured lust spoken in a thresh
For my there is no diplomacy when
The primal speaks acclaimed the flesh

First Time Etiquette

He knew to touch me with
The diplomacies of a first time
Yet it was all he promised it would
Be on our sensually private rhymes

The repertoire of his caresses took us
to a new spectrum of total euphoria
where we were consecrated as one
and brought to a most perfect Eutopia

Until Then

This envelope holds the millage travelling
poem of the love, I am attempting to convey.
Following poetical instincts my pen can help,
but to yield into inspiration and obey.

I can say I love you, countless times
But instead I remain in yearn to show you,

Physically, emotionally and spiritually
The things I crave to give you and do.

Because now, half of me belongs to you
I will endure my internal incompleteness
Building our nest until you come to me, with
Actions, followed by emotional lexical fitness.

Until then, let our love be written in the scrolls
Of time, as we wait for that moment to come.
Let us exchange in rhyme our feelings
Until the chariot of time brings you home.

5 LUST IN LOVE

The Alchemy of Equinox

Lost in this lustrous mirage,
I slumber within the dream
that cradles my fantasy.

Breaking the equinox, we crochet our souls
into a scarlet thread of frenzied caresses.
There, delicately and skillfully
his hands bind us as one.

Swooned by the ecstatic alchemy our flesh
I hear angelic harped tunes
 blessing our communion.

The ecliptic hallucination of our union
feeds the carnality of my deepest wants.

There in a moment within eternity
I feed on the bread of your flesh,
savoring all of its flavors
and loosing myself in their trance.

There between lurking imagination
And the prowling myths of reality
I embrace the crescent solstice of our union.

Passively and submissive
I surrender to the implosion
of rhythmic dancing hips and melted hearts.

Claiming me completely yours,
you impress your mark upon me.
Zealously we merge as one exalting
and glorifying the ecstasies of fantasy
that have brought us together.

-Figment of imagination?
Perhaps

-Inexplicable premonitions?
Indeed

As wading just like the sun,
this ardent hysteria of swollen desire
awakes me to see

I am truly in your arms.

Lustrous Voyage - An Erotica

She wears nothing but a panty,
just the way he likes it;
pacing through the room,
she summons his concealed attention.
His pants fill with aroused excitement
and sensual anticipation.
His masculine reflexes are clearly noticed
stimulating her into cold sweats.

Reciprocal lust is shared at a glance.
Body language becomes intense
and exotically graphic.

Every movement is well coordinated
by their engaging seduction game.
Her hard nipples spring like flowers
at the warmth of his breath.
They blossom in his mouth feeding him
the lotus of its sweetness.

Her hands travel softly through
the paradise of his body
as if wanting to discover and
conquer his whole flesh.
Her caress paints goose bumps
in his skin,
telling a story of the sensuality
her touch arouses in him.
Their foreplay dance is like
a hurricane harbor
and the peace in the middle

of the storm's eye, all at once.

There,
were the ambiance is serene
yet intense,
his body sets in motion to the journey
towards her inside.
She welcomes his masculinity
with a red carpet of desire.
He is further aroused by the greeting.

He knows he is home.
She knows she has brought him home.

There, within her bosom
he finds rest after the magnificence
of their ecstatic voyage.

Bedchamber's Decor

Etiquette and decorum,
with all modesty I say,
like any rules are meant to be broken.

The forthrightness of words
can be delicately disguised
but never masked.

Tenacious and unrelenting
the wants between one's crutch
can't be gagged
by the lofty rules of a social strata.

Indiscretion?
"Maybe so!"

A true lady allows herself a
gently woo.
A true lady follows the courting rules
imposed by civilization.

Ideations of whom?

Aren't men allowed the imprudence
of a mistress?
Perhaps two...
Isn't that socially acceptable?

Oh, I see

the philosophy of proper decorum
applies only to the females.
"Oopps! To the ladies, I should say".

Taboo is for a lady to seek
sanctuary in her carnal desires.

Bedchambers behaviors...
-Just another rule to be broken.

Frenzied Melody

I surrender to the tune within me
and let my hips dance to the rhythm of our passion.
Softly submissive I'm entranced
by the melody of the piano keys.

Desire flows through our veins like rivers of sound
as we move to the tenders notes of seduction!

Only you take me there

-where melody squirms between satin and silk sheets.
-where your touch is a harmonious submission
and where my feelings are entwined to each note.

Laying on my back,
I beckon after you and a frenzied crescendo.

-There, relentless notes are in parallel rhythm
with the silhouettes and shadows on the wall.

Only you take me there

where shadows also dance on wall

when we make love.

Sapphire Unrestraint

While hearkening the flamenco
song of nature
we kneel to the promise
of the incandescent ardor
that thralldomly makes me yours.

Enlaced by synchronized tongues
I can't toil with the bondage
of your kiss,
nor with the crystallized
luminescence of your sensuality.

Worship me
as I worship you!

Pearled specs of rain merge
with the sweat of our fleshly urges,
with the letch flickering dazzles
lighting the penumbra canopy
of the sapphire flair above.

Your hands delve quite
inquisitively searching the
adventurous destination
of the yen
roaring for your touch.

Touch me
as I crave to touch you!

The serene harbor of these
drudgery moments is the precious
chosen submission
my neck is shackled to
yet the incessant quest of our
unrestraint encounters.

In the mystic depths of reality

the fragrance of your silk is my
bondage and the clasping hold
of your hands is my release.

Make me your slave
as I claim you my freedom!

Thoughts of Touch

I love the way
your finger traces my back
with such tender comfort
after we make love

I love the way
your fingers loosen my curls
with such toying boyish nature

But when you hold my face
to kiss me,
I am lost in a most perfect
trance,
where all that matter is
you, I and the moment

I love the way
your hands touch me whole
leaving me satiated
yet yearning for more

I love the way my mind replays
every stroke and every sensations
you inspire and arouse in me

Thought upon thought
and touch upon touch
I just love the way
you make me feel

She Owns Me

Submersed in her coquettish
erotism,
I taste her whole,

no curve unturned,
no grotto unexplored.

I am submersed in the indulgent
wanton of her intoxicating vintage

lost in the acoustic notes
of a Spanish guitar
with rapturous exhilaration.

Softly, she whispers my name
ponderously staring me in my eyes,
feeding me the ambrosial
madness that only she
can make me feel.

And when she idolatrizes me
from within her knees

and asks me;
"Is this how you like it?"
I am further lost in her,

flowers crown spring,
torrents of mystique and magic
flow alive through me.

And I close my eyes
fearing she may see,
she owns me!

Gaze Me Answered

eyes of conspiracy
silently call his name

with the ardent hypnosis
 of a single glance

while fixed in the docile intoxication
of their topaz
he falls into an unrestrained drift
following their gleam
into a reminiscent beacon
of curious warmth

with a coyly
momentary glimpse
they can read his most vulnerable
yearnings
leaving him completely exposed

innocuously her stare
can exhilarate his heart
and leave him breathless

yet he passively yields
to their mesmerizing mystique
and surrenders
to their innocently sensual call,

for there
at the edge of a glance
he knows
he has found
the one he has been waiting for

Explore The Lands!

Decipher the evocative tenderness
of my terrain's riches.
Dare to climb the mountains
of my body and reach my summit.
I am earth, soil and land fields
for you to rip and harvest.

Listen to the muffled moans of the
dormant volcano only you awaken.

Be sustained by the flaunted
erotic nature of my lotus.
I am the arousal avalanche
between our two grottos.

Explore all that lies beneath
the sky, all that I am.
Heed to dusk seductress pleas
as they wield you into dawn.
I am the moon and
the sun birthing from firmament.

Decipher,
listen
and explore me
for I am life!

Sensuous Fluidity - Senryus

showered reflection
hands on blissful momento
it is all a game

liquid ecstasy
passion becomes a sweet smile
he touches me whole

fluidity flows
his touch rallies my wet skin
Elysian instant

Kiss After Kiss

scavenge me
drink my consent
I'm meant to be kept
so drink me as part
of you
kiss after kiss
limitlessly indulgent
rolling dices

we are each other's
yen and vices
scavenge me
grip me hard
and in a missionary
hold and embrace
nibble after nibble
bliss after bliss
kiss after kiss
scavenge me
consentingly
gallop my youth
with your tender
acumen and touch
and kiss after kiss

Burlesque Eloquences

listen pass the controversies
of these words

set aside the conventionalisms
of choices and even prudency
for just a little;

while the beguile allure of this
verb eloquently convinces you
to let me touch you

(((no)))
am not an eloquent harlot
yet I crave to touch you like one

-casting spells with poetry full lips
of oral endeavors

let me inherently survey the
philosophies of your internal
explorations

while sipping your sweat
and loosing myself inside you

and you inside me

mumble colloquialism of
conglomerated words

while I gently sway in waves
of pleasure the goods between
my legs

let me spread with legs up high
so you can reach me,

really reach the orgasmic core
that ignites ecstasy

as I melt underneath you
breathing the missionary scent
of your flesh

Give into these burlesque interludes
of poetry
just one time

one!
for I want you more
than words can say

My Lover

You are anesthetic caresses
taming hunger pain
at the delicate disturbance
of wee slumber hours.

Villainously you steel my rest;
replacing it with the responsive
blooming ascension of your
chivalry.

You are the journey
and destination I travel
following begging eyes

with intoxicating abandonment.

Maddeningly you are a
copulation explosion
disquietly exuding
the outcome of dulcet
moments.

You are
a mystery to decipher,
a new riddle with each touch
the challenge of rhythmic
adherent flesh.

You are my lover!
Powerless Submission Erotica

An explicitly beaconing smile
is the first sign of his intentions.

Licking his lips
he silently beseeches

a sensual supplication as his
solicitous glace interlock
with her compliant stare.

She slowly paces towards him
concealing the urgency
that rushes through her veins.

Gently
he brushes her hip with an
abundantly harden yet gentle
caress

as her cavernous grotto
conspires accordingly.

Lips become a reciprocated
nectar journey
and coy nuzzled strokes.

Resting over a bedded petal altar,
she drifts into a shimmering light

/of submission/

while he worships her
from within her inner legs,
nourished by the liquid intensity
of his labor.

Generously pleasing
he responds to her call
and travels north to her lips
where she also savors
the char taste of this blazed
communion.

Hovering fairies sprinkle
yearning dust of revived lust

as spellbound by the fantasy
of their magic her bewitching
emerald eyes

wordlessly implore for more

/for his exuberant hardness. /

Courteously and overzealously
he complies taking her

into Elysium
again and again

Unrivaled Glade of Night

Amiss vaporous distance of crepuscular lust
we are only a kiss away

under a nocturnal glade of constellations
I yearn to make her mine

About to witness our gentle consummation
is the sacred tent of sky.
-curiously prying

The lustration chamber of grass
is the bed of our passion,
from where I see the moon eclipsed
by the sweet gleam of her eyes,
begging me to undress the prudence gown
that clothes her trembling innocence.

Merging with the faint song of crickets
her pristine voice coyly begs me
to touch her,
while spreading her mysterious seas
for me to cruise.

And I,
I sail into a deciphering journey
with my fingers, traversing the waves
of her tidal desires.
-Diving deep into the core of her virgo.

Trembling, swelled and busting with bliss
she cries out for my masculinity
with feverish whispering moans:

((((Give it to me!))))

Soft and ever so gentle
I enter the censured portal of her
virtue worshiping the unrivaled throne
of her body.

My Venus passionately weeps
the drowsy ache of first time
gushing nectar in a monotone moan,
again and again,
begging for more, drenching my
pilgrimage erection.

From within the temple of night

and our bedding prairies
I make her the queen of my empire
as brazen trumpets announce my arrival
at the gates of heaven's climax
where she has taken me.

At the gateway of rapture, I avow
by the azure wings of night
that she is

forever mine!

Benedictine Requite

enthralled in seraphs
harped tunes
he baptizes me with
his masculine
countenance

with each stroke
I am blessed
with Elysium's grace
and rapture

I give into my
capricious affections
with the coquette
aura of sensuality

diving into his body
dancing like a goddess
bestowing him bliss

reciprocating
the effervescent pleasures
of the flesh

our erotic warbles
fill the atmosphere
with the bemoaning echoes
of this Benedictine

hermitage
in compassed
with the harp melodies

where winged chariots
whirr across heaven

with devouring ecstasy
yet he hushes my lips

suspending silence in fate
and thanking me
for requiting
the oral caresses

with the eloquent
language
of our baptismal
communion

6 LOSING - LOVE MELANCHOLIES

Winded Ballad of Ebon Nights

Winded ballad of ebon nights
What do you wish to speak to me?
-That I lose in whistles and caresses
And is so curiously toilsome.

Winded ballad of ebon nights
You drape in winged chariots
Over spacious landscapes
In dialogue with me.
-like the tickles of a lovers
Warbling to my ear.

Winded ballad of ebon nights
You tussle in voices by chambered
Windows extinguishing the
Silence of somber tranquility
And in barren echoes you urge him
To say:

(((((I love you!)))))

Winded ballad of ebon nights
You bring loveless lovers to me
And bed us in breviary of flashed
Caresses and brief communions
And speak in body languages,
Yet leave empty and used.

Winded ballad of ebon nights
Other times you bring the soft scent
Of lavender and chamomile serenity
And baptize me in the glorious
Momentum of stillness and sound
Sleep.

Winded ballad of ebon nights,

Darken echoes and angelic voices,
Yin and Yang of onyx hours
Speak to me in ancient rites
And mantras and tell me:
Where has my love gone?

Life's Cycles

Victimized
by the infidel cataclysm
of her actions
I feel a shanked flank pain.

/I lay breathless/

The opulent tossing winds
of our 30 springs
gust away
leaving me ponderously cold
next to an empty bedside.

Hazardous recollections
are but cynical muse of my
blistering grief
a deflowering of inspiration;

she took it with her
when she left.

/poetry now is
but the foreign language
that never was/

And I,

a mendicant bargainer
curse destiny
for gloating evolution
at my cost.

I sometimes sit
at the edge of her bed side

and reach over the night table
to glance at the photographed
collage of past.

/only to catacomb into
depression
and a ravenous anger/

Better days sometimes
visit with me
as I forbid
these romping realizations
from further cannibalizing
my spirit.

/Acceptance comes
soft like the morning dew
flashing alpha and tossing omega/

Sometimes I survive;
sometimes I live.

But there is always
that spinning cycle of grief
toying with the man that I am.

180 Degrees of Truth

-Though a premonition had already visited me
at the realms of intuition, I was still deceived
by the subtleties of so called relationships.
No more staring blankly at what is chosen to
be believed. Today the cliché of actions is
obnoxiously louder than any other concepts.
And so are the revelations.
No pretenses,
just self-validation.
I am worth sincerity and so much more.
Nope, I am not selling myself short any longer.
The sale price tag has expired along with my
trust.
Resolved into one hundred and eighty degrees

of separation, today you become something
of the past, just another lesson to extract
knowledge from
Today our bond was abbreviated to fraud
opening the door to the severances I walk
away from.
And as I cross its threshold, I come to
realize that I am just freeing myself from
the claws of the enemy and I can't help
to be grateful for it all, even though it hurts.

Toxic Rivalries Farewells

My rival wears no lipstick
Nor does it have feminine enthralling curves
Of predestined claims

My rivals name is skepticism
Your hesitancies are but a pack of wolves
Devouringly making these feeling their prey

Thus I hide behind a fortress of guards
Take these one-sided offerings
And subconsciously set conscious
Travels into a maze
Of forgetting thresholds

There, I can heal from the poisoning toxins
Of your reluctance and absorb the placebos
Of distance and silence
There in that final place
There is obviously no need for words
There is no need for goodbyes
Even though its over

Tangible Indulgences

tangible indulgences...
sweet and sour
especially while borrowed
they still mystify

insensitively sensitive
understandings are clear

you are an oxymoron of
an abrasive placebo
madness enslaved
emancipated in desire

of reciprocated explorations
diplomatically beseeching
of course

oh, but you leave me thirsty
and fruitlessly bonded
to surrogate dreams
and affections alike

willowing in promises
and lonely autumnal dusks
soon turning to insurgent
white and to a bitter cold
no wool blanket can tame

but you my fire
are the greatest and sweetest
lie I ever pretended to believe
so I burn

and still want behind any
shields of concealment

ready every night
for the wheel of fortune
of your whims
I wait

for you to rip
our tangibly achy
but so borrowed
palpable indulgences

Unable to Love

-just like that time expired
vanishings of what was once aspired
selective silence was a choice
and he became lost in a muted voice
consequentially, time moved immutably
thus perceptions are now inscrutably
all that is left is an indifferent distance
apathy born from your resistance
so now lick the wounds of your repressions
for all you have left is but retrospection
I hope your hurt is worth your decision
and you've learned it was not what you envisioned
on that note I still wish you the best
if love comes again I hope you can manifest

Soap Bubbles Release

When you kissed me,
you brought out the little girl within
me to blow soap bubbles onto
the air, and make wishes
exhaling dandelions.

You brought back the innocence
of believing in love again.
-The wishing, the wanting,
the peace and euphoria,
all the same.

I felt you, God sent
but the delusions and illusions
of love and lust can be blinding
and I got caught off guard by a wave
much like a mirage.

Though, I love you
and am eternally grateful
for being my soul's placebo,
I release you with the same
innocence you woke and I received

you with.
I release like soap bubbles onto
the air.

Nothing To Reminisce About

You were
a long term concealment.
-Countless scraps of
poetry to read and
reminisce upon

Just Ask

Ask your mirror
what at my kisses?
Lie, like you miss me not...
Ask your mirror
and your mind too
does it think of me
when you least expected it?
Ask your mirror

Bone Marrow Felt Absence

I am missing you, tonight
your absence is fight or flight
in the tracks of melancholy
run where, If I find you in every melody
every song, every lyric, every verse
an absence too real cannot be rehearsed
you are a damn crescendo in my mind
an ache so deep to conjugate or rhyme
though temporary, this distance is so narrow
it even sits in my blessed bone morrow
time is uncooperative and rampant
and hurtfully stagnant
let this melancholy retire to its chambers
where I'm warmed by blankets of disclaimers
and where the obsessions and its willows

don't cut deep me but rest on feathery pillows
instead I will seek you in my dreams
where your green eyes beacon me in gleams
so let me slumber under tender covers
see you in my dreams my tender lover

Long Lost Osmosis

We used to be close.
I would think
and telepathically thoughts
were transferred
from my mind
to his mind
to his pen
/and vice versa/

The blanket of lilies
his caresses were
are now distant terrains of indifference,
the halted silence of a sworn monk
When did we lose the impressions
and expressions of our muses?

It was long ago, any of us wrote a love poem.
-you know?

The preambles of then,
the instantaneous projection of our union,
and the promulgations of commitment
are the obituaries of the feelings that
once bounded us.
/aren't poetry now/

-Just the walls of oblivion's pit
encasing a constant free fall
of verbal wounding exasperations.
/nope, definitely not poetry/

Inspiration these days are a conundrum
of complicating inquiry, and undeciphered
reason or even excuses for the loss.

But infliction no matter the cost
or the number of spins.

Dissolved by osmotic powers
We are no longer close.
Telepathy, love and muses are long gone
from his mind
from my mind
and from our pens

In His Mind

he had memorized every
detail of her beauty

the way her jet black hair softly
fell on her shoulders
and the sweet scent of patchouli
he breathed every night
when he watched her sleep

the way she would summon
his manhood with a single glance
the way she could read his depth
the way he felt every time
she pierced her greens upon him

the softness of her facials
expressions and the sensual feel
of it resting upon his chest

the way her lips mischievously
curled when she wanted him
the flavor of her tongue on his
the way they playfully journeyed
his body

all he had to do was close his eyes
and she'd be right there

she's been gone for three years
now but he still knows how to

bring her to life
by just closing his eyes

Red Roses and Wine

It was long ago

When love bounteously
Spoke the languages of
Red petals and the bliss
Of vintage soft lips

Reverberations
And vanishing echoes
Of what capriciously is
Long gone are
the whispers left behind

As some god has them
Sequestered
And replaced by implacably
Forbidden wants

It was long ago

When I respired the scent
I pray to be reconciled with

-Long ago

Since the impeccable feel
Of maddening chardonnay
Tongue strokes tasted my flesh

Sobriety and
Indiscreet wilted lonesome
Emotions of an empty
Muse bottle is the repertoire
Of my poetry these days

Life is a sequence
Of expectant days

Yearning the intoxication
Of manly hands filled
With roses
To zeal my life once again

Dousing Squall Farewell

Sedulously destiny planned
our farewell with idyllic precision,
even the sky turned sullen gray
and sadden rite.

Spiritless
in the arms where I belong,
I embrace the vessel of change
that comes to take you
away from me.

For it is immutable like God's will.

Even the pelting sounds of
raindrops have lost composure
and feel dream forsaken.

Why must you part from me
my love?

You take my soul with you
my darling!

Care for it and guard it as you
would a small child and
bring it back to me someday.

Under the drenching canvas of
our farewell, hold me like you did
on our first embrace.

Filled with expectation
and trembling with love.

Make me feel those butterflies,

so this pain can be momentarily
tamed with your promise of return.

Kiss me one last time
under this tormenting dousing squall
for you leave me broken and lost.

Oh, so lost!

-But with a slight tantalizing hope
that you will return someday!

Empty Ambrosia Chalice

Your quenching ambrosia came
to the perched nomad I was,
unexpectedly and unpredictably
to fill the impassive grotto
of my internal void
and exile the melancholy that
claimed me its personal property.

You became the promulgation
of my fate and a creed
with the raging river force
that would sweep me away.

Overtaken by the currents,
we flooded the silken valleys of
pleasures, emotions and all that
I thought was love.

But the chalice soon was empty,
and my wine tasting lips
weren't enough to keep you
inebriated.
The intoxication of my touch soon
became a slight hazy feeling.
But I didn't know

And your brimmed dismissal
came like inopportunist winds

of a malicious tornado breaking
the branches of the tree
with so much love we had planted.
It came with a dark somber morning
and a thunderous roar.

and you are now gone.

Now, I cry like a foolish child.
I cry to the tune of sad violin
decrescendo and try to erase the
promising calligraphy, you inked
on the parchment of my soul.
As your lingering velvet caresses
and your memories
are an unrequited recollection
of what I thought it was love.

Tell Me Madam

Tell me madam,

who left your vascular
crimson emotions hemorrhaging
and made your womanly spirit
almost vanish?

Did he take you on a crusade
of promises just to leave them
lying on soil
just like dead corpses?

Did he carve the translucent
gypsum of caresses upon your
alabaster flesh to then
blemish it with the scars
of abandonment?

Tell me madam,

what is the ransom for your love?

Do not let my expectations
of an answer drip like water
between my fingers.

I sense the unease of my query.
I discern how someone's ice age
machistas ideals may have
left you hurt and wounded.

Tell me madam,

can you see I bring not
the seed of unfulfilled promises,
not I wish to saw trees of lies.

I just want to rip
a new beginning for you.

I crave to paint
a smile on your face.
I just want to anchor the ship
of my love in a moment of pure
marine stillness for you to see
the vast ocean of feeling
I hold for you.

Tell me madam,

what is the ransom for your love?

7 IN-LOVE WITH NATURE

Temptress Primavera of Romance

Faint like the melody from a music box
springs song begins to softly play.

Each tune carries a shade of green
soft lime,
mint,
emerald,
olive
forest and more...
-All gallantly dress the naked barks
autumn and winter yielded to past.
-All rugged the soil from horizon to
horizon which forgotten lay nude.

Labor and birth
a new season is finally here.

Temptress leaves dance at the rhythm
of a fresh breeze as if inviting the sun
to shine a kiss upon.

Aromatically flirtatious dandelions
come out to play and engage in the
sensual drafty dance of
the brand new air.

Maidens blue birds,
sparrows
and red cardinal
plumage their way into the sunlit ball
while gallantly their suitors
build their love nests
with courting songs to sweep them along.

In delicate white silk gowns
voluptuous ladies levitate
the powder blue skies assuring close

proximity to chivalrous
warmth of the sun.

The voluminous river bank currents
waltz with the solicitous courting season
that allures them enthralled.

Walking along,
I welcome this panoramic harmony of
colors,
scents
and romance

which plays from within
spring's musical box.

Allegory to Nature

I
The day mimics life from dawn till the dusk
of my today. Each sight brings a new allegory
to our union. As dawn brings the promised
blessing of a new morning,
the sun kisses me awake to these feelings
that gleam for you. Hot and misty like
morning dew I sense you wet and warm upon
me, kissing me awake just like the rays
filtering my windows.

II
This Saturday morning slowly grows from
a leisure hammock swing to an incredible
sight above. I see our dreams levitate and
fly like a leaf in the wind whirling and
twirling at the rhythm of our love.
They travel far to the horizon of a blissful
future where firmament blue tapes off to
the turquoise of the far away sea.
-Saluting the perfectly woven fabric of each
and every cloud filling the cosmic powder
blue.

III
Noon's blazing gold gleams down directly
into the patio set where we nourish our bodies
with food and our souls with glances,
touch and those perfectly unspoken three words
I see in your eyes. We have rooted together
as the great emerald bloomed oak that shades
us now, as you promise me eternity beyond
death. The bowed assurance of your words
merges with the acoustic soft whisper of this
 breeze that caresses our spirits renewed.

IV
Wild flowers aroma beckons my glance to
their rainbow ballet. I breathe the pollinated
fragrance of the serene afternoon. Holding
hands we pace the margined silver iridescence
of the calmed bank where the lily pads
placidly rest upon. There you quench my
aqueous thirst with a soft kiss and fill me
with desire as your hands travel my curves
with warmth appeasing my shivering flesh.

V
Time flies by between coruscating kisses
and the touch of the birthing crimson,
scarlet and orange sky. In ceremonious
reverence to our union the sun waves goodbye
and hides by the mountain side as the day
collapses into dusk. The willows house the
owls, the darkness hides bats, and the green
summon the crickets, and the dusk directs
their choir to the harmonious nightly song.

VI
The canopy of navy draws a constellation
of luminous incandescent muse and filter
through the awning of night with the vision

of a new moon. Your hands caress me into
metaphor. Your lips kiss me like the soft
grass that blankets our nakedness. You cast
your manly desires upon the ballad of my
flesh. You scribble us into the scrolls of
communion where in allegory to nature
you disguised us as poetry.

Firmament Bodies

Under a silvered blue horizon,
a waning moon
and a late sun set
the night begins to birth.

Un-rivalry, both bodies
in firmament witness
the lover's waywardness.

Mischievous they give into
the appeal of the balcony breeze.
Not by happenstance
but by choice
they eviscerate their carnal yearning.

Within the realms of reality
they disregard
the chanced bystanders above.

Intricately they partake
of their fleshful moment
where no one
but the sun and the moon
can judge.

Super Nova

Enlightening and refocusing while
 I hold stars in my hands
 They show me the path
 The glisten upon my journal

I am inspired by celestial bodies
And by the greatest morning star
I am where there is no absence of light
For I am it energetically synergic
There within is where dreams are manufactured
And where work host the successes
Of quantum delights of illuminations
Transformed into materializations
At last

Rain for Poets

Woven macramé of gray clouds
impressionably soft and tender
yet engorged speed race
the horizon as in a hurry
to nestle poets.

-Slowly unraveling pearled
droplets into a streaming
temple of essential beauty
and perfection

while muses creep under
bed covers sharing playful
moments of affection.

A sense of languor burns
in the fire place filling
the ambiance of scented
warmth and hickory bark.

Inexorable inspiration births
from singing chimes carefully
played by the fingers of a
wet wind.

Streets are cleansed,
the natural emerald is nurtured,
and spirits renewed by the
liquid blessing of an eastern
sky.

The creaking wooden floor,
the pelting on the roof,
the drumming on the window pane
and the thundering crescendos
are a perfectly orchestrated
symphony of nature for any poet
to be inspired from.

<u>One with A Natural Love</u>

Today, I want to erase solace
from the vocabulary of my life
and enjoy the caress of the sun
as I walk the meadows of experience.

Today, I want to be touch by the
ethereal presence of the wind whispering
in my ears and blowing in my hair
as he is a most sweet companion.

Today, I want to embrace the earth
and fill my eyes with its emerald verbs,
and the growth from soil as I my bare
feet become one with nature.

Today, I want to make love to dusk
and let the orange ablaze sky burn my flesh
and fill me with its sensual energy
as I climax into temperate implosion.

Today, I want to strive
to love me whole
screaming out loud I am alive!

Fall Morning Enrapture

Canvassed by rapturous
sunlight and lost in morning
blue jays orchestra tunes

hesitancy lucidly drifts away
with the thrusting of chimerical
wings and your hands.

Desires pastures is a herbage
bed for us, where in your arms
I can feel savage palpitations
of lust beat upon my breast
rhapsodizing this will of mine.

-sweetly imprisoned
my resolve yields pleading for
more and submerging in wanton...

Expectant my lips beseech your
nectar and claim your orphan heart
mine as you nervously ignited like
lustful marigolds burn under my
worshiping hips.

Dance and melt to the chortling heat
of an autumnal morn,
dance my love!

I am a Tree

I
I am a tree,

now naked of leaves as fall has
stripped me bare.
My trunk speaks the tale of
my life, my bark is a rough
as my experiences have made it.
My roots are sunken upon the soil
of a strong foundation.
My branches reach for the sky,
yet they cannot touch the celestial
treasures I fathom.
The breeze has caressed me with the
tenderness of brand new lovers
but has also tugged and pulled me

with the rugged experiences of a
temperate mother nature.

II
I am a tree,

waiting for the frost of winter
and its bridal gown of its first snow
drop.
Resting in home's lawn I will wear
Christmas light and seasonal
ornaments while Mr. Snow Man
melts away.
Mother nature will hang diamond
stalactites icicles from my bark
and make me pretty.

III
I am a tree,

embracing the new born emerald
tones of a birthing spring.
I bathe with morning dew and am
caressed by tender sun rays looking
above to hovering blue jays and
red robins nesting their kindred
on me.
I will look down and will
find myself surrounded by wild
marigolds and will breathe the scent
of fresh cut green grass.

IV
I am a tree,

the base of kids playing tag
as I ponder their playful innocence.
I will be the canvas of a young's first
summer kiss and a concealing shelter
to their love anew.
I am the
shade sheltering the still in love

grandparents swinging on a porch swing.

V
I am a tree,

breathing, growing, living.
But I am only a tree!

Tequila Haikus

inebriating flor
hummingbirds hover nectar
nature's tequila

random yucca sprouts
swirl and dance caressed by gust
grow wild in my yard

blooming casaba
mother sorcerer magic
wrapped emerald lush

bashfully glowing
innocent pearled soft petals
unparalleled bud

untamed white budding
nature fruit abloom allure
patriarch blossom

Prelude of Change

chills of fall sneak upon
the scenery,
autumn becomes real right
before our eyes

the lake's surface no longer
wear ripples
but a crystalline sheet of ice

the leaves wear yellows
burgundies
reds.
even the colors speak
a tale of change

deer hide
seeking shelter from the
days to come

we all seek to tame
the cold that proceeds fall

the seasons run wild
stampeding one after the next
just in time

yesterday
everything was myrtle and forest

even the streets
know fall is here

the warmth of summer days
are but memories

the drive home
is full of naked trees
a blue sky
and a warm sun

even the cloud hide
as the season begins
to claim its time

time joins reality
immutable
absolute

beautiful sceneries
for one who never
befriended cold

but fell in love
with the beauty of fall

Autumn's Poetical Elixir

The rooster's morning song
brings muses
in a musical promise
along with the sweeping aroma
of fallen leaves.

Inspiring the poet within!

The embosomed surrounding
is the elixir aroma of
poetical dialect.

Naked trees,
brown bark
and graceful branches
fill the countryside
like the placid morning mist

Enthusing the poet within!

while the prismatic colors of
fall create a visual imagery
of autumn's bewitching
magnificence by the roadside.

Motivating the poet within!

The tranquil venture
and the bloody hues adorning
the ground are simply
nestle ground
for this fall poem to birth.

Blessing the poet within!

Visual Nightingales

Abed gazing upon the abstract scenery
and its magnificent splendor I am bliss.

Paradise collages its self upon the suburbia
I call home
simply nudging me to count the visual
blessings pouring for heavens window.

The mischievous nocturnal beauty
filters through my eyes

and walks to the core of my soul leaving
inexhaustible dazzle traces of the
constellation spectra smiling from above.

Vaporous dusted gray giants float upon
the horizon reflecting like a mirror upon
the serenity of the hand of the lake,

while abed,

stillness cradles my spirit and soothes
my being.

The chimes serenade the innocent
nightingales of early fall's tender breeze
walking along with me through my visual
journey.

The intangible songs of night and
the ethereal brightness of a maiden moon
are beckoning visual and auditory echoes
of crafted heartwarming art.

Lost on the gleaming grace caressing the
rosaceous field I am joined in slumber cradles

by a most exquisite night!

Nebbish Russet Tones of Fall

Puerilely and nebbish
autumn chills caress
the new russet leaves
giving a sneak preview
of its crimson collage;

while nestled by the
new season,
I walk along
with vagabond clouds
enjoying its sight.

A faint pine scent fills
my lungs and my eyes
of tossed confetti cones
landing innocently
by my feet
unable to demise
nor deny Summer's good bye.

Irenic and calmed
the venting winds
engrave the autumnal return
of scarlet pastures
and landscapes
for all to see.

Ah! Fall is here!

The sleeping season
of crunching leaves
doesn't expiate,
nor makes amends.

Although absolutely beautiful,
ineffably,
its presence is exorably inevitable,
while like pheromones
its autumnal passion
provokes poetry and verb.

Yes,
fall is finally here!

Nirvana's Dawn

He kisses me golden,
sneaked through the window
to burgle my sleep
and bestow upon me
the "every day new blessings"
promised by the Verb.

I inhale the misty heaven
of green's dew!
The nectar glory
of a brand new day
filters my nostrils
making way to my soul.

It is so early,
even the volcano's cone rests
still asleep,
away
yet so close from sight.

Nirvana shines through
my window pane.

Dawn awaken feathered Mozart's
play the melodies
of their celestial limitless freedoms

while I rejoice.

Jealous ebony crows
salute the sun as do I.

Ah!
I am alive
and marked by the insignia
of His beauty and His might.

Yes
It is God Himself
simply saying
Good Morning!

CHAPTER 8 BECAUSE LOVE IS RAISING AWARENESS

Cherubim's Cradle

Mathew John is my name, says the nurse lady.
Yet I hear everyone calling me the meth baby.
Here in Neo-Natal my bed is an incubator.
I thought, I would have a cherubim's cradle.

But blatantly, mommy has a fatal disease
and though she tried, just couldn't resist.
She said, she would be back in a couple of days.
But instead she's been lost is a methadone's haze.

The doctors are trying to wean me from the drugs.
I just want my mommy; I just want to be hugged.
A child protective worker spoke to the nurse
I heard her telling him I am getting worse.

I'm having seizures and I'm in too much pain.
I fear my body they can no longer maintain.
They say my mommy is just a meth head
that instead of life she cursed me to death.

Feeling weaker and weaker I'm waning away.
My spirit is leaving my little sick body astray.
Without seeing mommy, I soon will be graven.
Without a kiss from her, I am going to heaven.

I am just one more tale of a true disputed polemic.
I am just one more tale of a wide spread epidemic.
Mathew John was my name, said the nurse lady.
-Simply, just one more forsaken methadone baby.

Springs and Cradles

Fourteen springs fell in love for the very first time
barely learning how love can be so sublime.

Under the peer pressures of being in love
she gives herself to her insisting beloved.

Knowing better they decide to use no protection;
all she bares in mind is to prove her affection.

Fourteen springs didn't see the future results.
-But they both knew better, they're both at fault.

Five months pregnant she becomes a statistic,
but lost in house games she can't be realistic.

He decides it's too much, he won't stick around.
But she thought his love was really profound.

Her dreams were not being a teen single mother
But to be a dad her beloved didn't even bothered.

Now fifteen springs her life is so depressing
yet she still sees her baby as a big blessing.

One More Awareness Tale

My name is Jane
and my sister's name is Beth.
We live in fear;
we are scared half to death.

See everything started
when mom passed away
He can't get it together
and our lives are disarrayed.

If he loses his temper
all hell will break loose
one of us is bound
to end up with a bruise.

The other day Beth spilled

her milk on the floor.
And he started yelling
he couldn't take it no more!

He got so angry
and hit us both with the belt
It was the worse pain
that I ever felt.

Dad is mad again;
so keep your voice down!
Hush little sister please
Don't make a sound.

Though we were quiet
dad came in the room
he started cursing
and beat us with the broom.

So we're going to bed
with hungry tummies.
God make it ok
give us back our mommy.

Why can anyone see
and make the law aware?
We are two little girls
tired of living in despair.

Please somebody help us
before is too late.
Before our daddy
makes a fatal mistake.

But our screams and pain
were ignored or unheard.
The neighbors knew
they just didn't care.

Today we're in heaven
and we hope you're aware
that there are still kids like
us still living in despair.

ABOUT THE AUTHOR

Iris Yanette Seda is a 46-year-old, Puerto Rican woman, mother of five and caretaker of her disabled father. She is and has always been passionate about poetry. -Ever since she can remember. She has always dreamed of sharing her poems in a book. And "Love Hieroglyphics" is her dream come true, it is that book. It is the manifestation of a dream, a prayer and passionate work. Though, she never stopped writing, she never pursued writing as a career either. It was mostly a hobby, an outlet, a therapeutic coping mechanism. Thus she acquired a Bachelors in Science in Human Services at Boricua College, NYC in 1992 making the Dean's List of 1992. She also attained certifications as: Insurance Agent, Phlebotomy, EMT, Biller and Coder. It was in her late thirties, that she discovered her passion for the medical field and a compassionate love and care for her patients and in intervals of time, she writes. In intervals of times, she crafted what she called her hieroglyphics of emotions. -an anthology of love poems.

"First book published at 46. Don't ever let age determine the outcome of your dreams. Let it inspire you to live, culture and re-create yourself. We are works in-progress, thus unfinished products."

Made in the USA
Columbia, SC
23 December 2017